WHY DO AIRPLANES HAVE SMALL WHEELS?

EVERYTHING YOU NEED TO KNOW ABOUT THE AIRPLANE VEHICLES FOR KIDS

CHILDREN'S PLANES & AVIATION BOOKS

BABY PROFESSOR

EDUCATION KIDS

Speedy Publishing LLC

40 E. Main St. #1156

Newark, DE 19711

www.speedypublishing.com

Copyright 2018

In this book, we're going to talk about the parts of an airplane. So, let's get right to it!

Airplanes are marvels of engineering. There are many different types of airplanes, but their basic parts are very similar.

Fuselage
(Body)

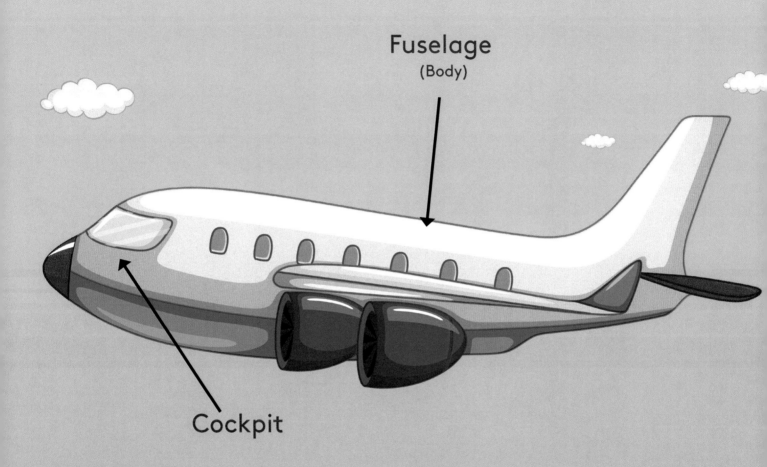

Cockpit

THE COCKPIT AND FUSELAGE

THE FUSELAGE

The part of the airplane that you enter if you are going to be a passenger and where your baggage is stored is called the fuselage. It's a long tube that tapers off at the back of the plane, the opposite end of where the cockpit is located. The wings are attached to the fuselage. The empennage, which is the airplane's tail, is also attached to the fuselage.

THE WINGS

The wings are complex and important structures on airplanes. The fuselage has wings connected to it on both sides. The wings create the lift that is necessary to get the aircraft into the air.

As far as wing positioning, there are two different types of aircraft. Some aircraft have their wings near the fuselage's top. These aircraft, the Cessna 162 is an example, are called high-wing aircraft.

CESSNA 162 SKYCATCHER

THE PIPER CHEROKEE IS AN EXAMPLE
OF A LOW-WING AIRCRAFT

If the wings are attached to the fuselage's bottom, then they are described as low-wing aircraft.

TERRAFUGIA

The Terrafugia Transition, a new experimental flying car, is an example of a low-wing aircraft. In all cases, the wing's front is described as its leading edge and its back is described as its trailing edge.

The wing is composed and supported by the structure of metal spars, which travel the length of the wing, and metal ribs, which are parallel to the fuselage and at right angles to the spars. There are also metal stringers that keep the wing's skin from bending. The outside skin of the wing is composed of fabric or aluminum or a composite of materials.

PILATUS PC-24

There are two very important types of structures on the wing's trailing edge: the aileron and the flaps.

FLAPS ON WING OF PLANE

IMAGE OF WING WHILE BRAKING

The purpose of these structures is to transform the wing's shape to increase or decrease lift for various stages of flight.

The Aileron

The aileron is located on the wing's tip on the wing's back edge. It's essentially an airfoil that is rectangular in shape. It rises up to disrupt the flow of air over the aircraft's wing. By doing so, the aileron makes the lift on one wing greater than the other, which makes it possible for the pilot to turn the aircraft. The ailerons are farther away from the fuselage than the flaps are.

The Flaps

Flaps are airfoils as well. They are also found on the wing's rear closest to the fuselage for each wing. The purpose of the flaps is to make the wing's surface area larger. This helps the airplane to have more lift for takeoff or for landing.

AN AIRPLANE WINDOW VIEW OF WING AND FLAPS.

There are many different types of flap designs depending on the aircraft. Some of the various types are plain, split, slotted, Fowler, and slotted Fowler.

EMPENNAGE

THE EMPENNAGE

The empennage is at the "tail end" of the airplane attached to the end of the fuselage. There are two main pieces on the empennage. They are the vertical stabilizer, which is described as the airplane's tail, and the horizontal stabilizer, which is similar to a stabilator.

The Rudder

The rudder is a portion of the vertical stabilizer. The pilot has foot pedals in the airplane's cockpit that control the rudder. By moving the rudder, the pilot can make the plane turn either left or right along its vertical axis.

Rudder

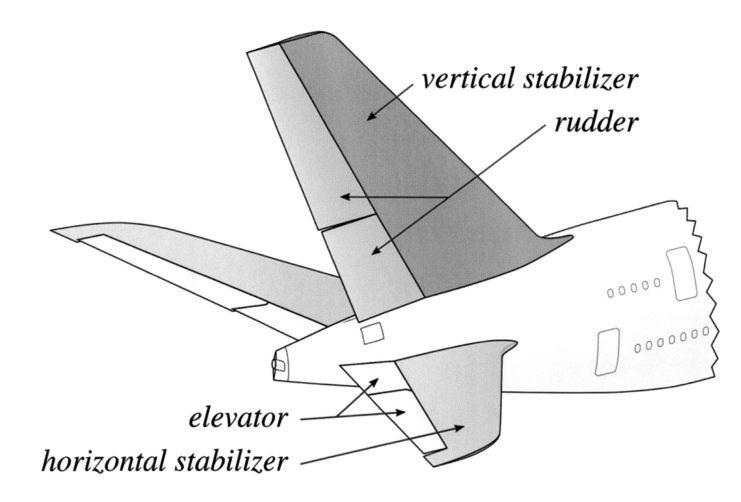

vertical stabilizer

rudder

elevator

horizontal stabilizer

The Elevator

The elevator runs almost the full length of the horizontal stabilizer's rear section. When the pilot pulls back on the yoke, which is located

in the cockpit, the elevator goes upward. This action forces the horizontal stabilizer to move down and the airplane's nose to go upwards.

The Trim Tab

The trim tabs are rectangular structures on the rear edge of the horizontal stabilizer. The pilot moves them gradually to make the aircraft simpler to maneuver. There's a trim tab under the rudder on the vertical stabilizer as well.

AIRCRAFT AILERON TRIM TAB DETAIL

MILITARY AIRPLANE VERTICAL STABILIZER

The Stabilator

Some airplanes have a stabilator. The stabilator is something like a horizontal stabilizer. However, it doesn't have an elevator. Instead, it's one large structure that has an anti-servo tab, which also acts as a trim tab. The anti-servo tab makes the controls seem heavier to the pilot, which for lighter planes gives them more stability.

THE POWERPLANT

Depending on the type of aircraft, the powerplant might be in the front of the fuselage or it could be located toward the airplane's rear. In aircraft that have more than one engine, the engines are typically positioned under the wings on both sides.

AIRPLANE POWERPLANT

The powerplant is what powers the craft. It is made up of the engine and its components, the propeller, and the aircraft's electrical system.

THE LANDING GEAR

The wheels on an aircraft are used for takeoff on the runway and for landing on the runway. Smaller airplanes have wheels that stay positioned ready for takeoff and landing at all times. Larger aircraft have wheels that retract into the body of the plane.

Once the aircraft has successfully taken off, these wheels, called the landing gear, are retracted. When the plane is about to land, the wheels come down again so that the plane can land on the runway.

The configuration of the wheels may be in a triangular arrangement with wheels under the nose of the plane and wheels at the back of the plane.

Originally, many types of airplanes had a conventional gear arrangement, which consists of two main wheels on the front and one single wheel in the back. This type of plane is sometimes described as a tailwheel or taildragger airplane.

The wheels for the landing gear often seem small based on the overall size of the aircraft, but they are engineered to take the weight and pressure of the plane.

There are also struts that attach the wheels to the airplane. There are many different types of struts. Here are the four main types:

- Rigid
- Spring Steel
- Bungee Cords
- Shock

Rigid Struts

Rigid struts were the original type of airplane landing gear. They simply attached the wheels to the airplane. If the touchdown was hard, the impact was transferred to the passengers. It wasn't long after that when new airplane designs were developed that had inflatable tires to help soften that impact.

WING STRUTS

Spring Steel Struts

Spring steel struts are the struts used in small planes like the Cessna. They are made of strong, somewhat flexible material and can take a beating. When the plane begins to touch down, the spring moves and flexes upward. It transfers the impact to the airframe and hopefully doesn't bend the plane in the process.

SPRING STEEL

Bungee Cords

Bungee Cords are a group of cords made from elastic that connect the airframe and the gear system. The elastic lessens the shock of the wheels hitting the ground. One of the most popular airplanes that uses this type of struts is the Piper Cub.

SHOCK ABSORBER

Shock Struts

Shock struts are the only type of struts that truly absorb shock. They use nitrogen or compressed air with hydraulic fluid to absorb the landing impact. These types of struts can be found on smaller aircraft, but they can also be found on larger jets.

These struts use a top cylinder that is attached to the airplane's body and also a bottom cylinder that's connected to the landing gear. The bottom cylinder slides in and out of the top cylinder.

THE COCKPIT

The cockpit is the command center of the aircraft. This is where the pilot and co-pilot sit to control the aircraft. Every aircraft is a little different in terms of the design of its dashboard and controls.

PILOTS IN THE COCKPIT

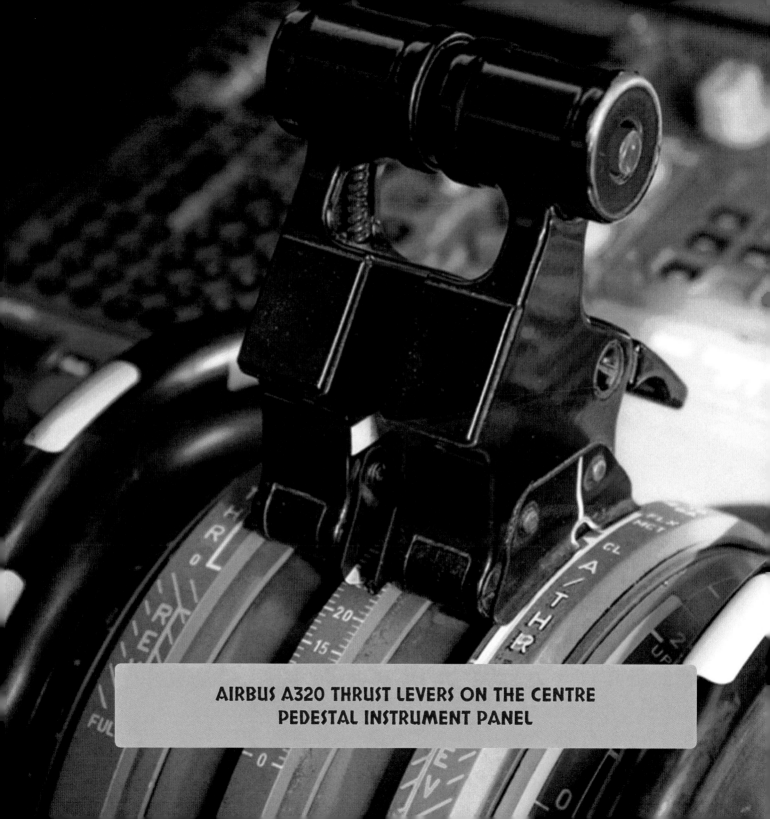

AIRBUS A320 THRUST LEVERS ON THE CENTRE
PEDESTAL INSTRUMENT PANEL

THE FOUR FORCES OF FLIGHT

There are four forces involved in the dynamics of flight.

- Thrust is the force that propels the plane forward through the use of the engines. It must overcome drag for the plane to fly.

- Lift is the force that is generated by the wings and other parts of the plane as it moves through the air. It needs to overcome weight for the plane to fly.

- Drag is the force that is produced by the friction of the air against the plane's forward motion.

Weight is the force that is generated by the gravitational pull of the Earth.

AIRCRAFT TAKES OFF FROM THE AIRPORT RUNWAY AT SUNSET.

SUMMARY

Today's aircraft have many different designs, but they all share some common parts. The fuselage stores the passengers and luggage. The powerplant contains the engine and electrical system. The landing gear contains the struts and the wheels, which often seem small based on the plane's size. Depending on the type of plane, some struts and wheels are always in the same position or move only to absorb impact, while others are designed to retract into the plane after takeoff. The wings and the empennage are vital to the lift and steering of the plane. The cockpit is where the pilot and co-pilot maneuver the plane from takeoff to landing.

Wilbur

Orville

The Wright Brothers created the first successful Airplane.

Now that you've read about the parts of an airplane, you may want to read about one of history's most famous pilots in the Baby Professor book: Where Has Amelia Gone To? The Amelia Earhart Story Biography of Famous People | Children's Women Biographies.

Visit

BABY PROFESSOR
EDUCATION KIDS

www.BabyProfessorBooks.com

to download Free Baby Professor eBooks
and view our catalog of new and exciting
Children's Books

Made in the USA
Monee, IL
10 April 2021